S0-EGS-091

Dee Etta

Having A Friend Is...

love
Darla

Having A Friend Is...

A Book About
the Meaning of Friendship
By Dean Walley

Illustrated by Toshiko Muto

Hallmark Editions

Having A Friend Is...

Having a friend is...
sharing your dearest possession.

It's thinking,

"Gee, I sure would like to go to the beach!"

at the very minute

when your friend comes in

with his under-water goggles

and says, "Scuba do?"

Having a friend is...

being under the weather together...

...and liking it!

Having a friend is...
acting so silly

that everyone says,

"Look at them!

Aren't they the silliest ever?!"

And sometimes
it's being very serious.

Having a friend is...

yawning a lot

and staying up very late

because you have so much

to talk about.

Sometimes

it's not saying anything

at all

because you don't need any words.

Having a friend
is being needed.

No matter how small you are

it's feeling tall...

...and no matter

how far apart you are

it's knowing you are close

in heart.

Having a friend is...
discovering something wonderful
and keeping it a secret...
just the two of you.

Every once in a while
having a friend is...
having a fight!

But pretty soon
you'll forget
about the whole thing.
That's just the way it is
when you have a friend.

Having a friend

can even be

      having a lot of fun together

doing something

      you've been putting off...

      like raking the leaves.

Having a friend is...
     walking around the block
          and running
               into an adventure...

...it's changing
tears to laughter

...and

it's bringing a special kind
of sunshine

to a rainy day.

Having a friend is...
like having a magic mirror
in which you can see yourself
as you really are.

It's feeling nice

and easy

and never mind the elbows ...

It's really being You
and knowing
your friend likes you that way
Best Of All!